Marketing in the Data Age

Linking Consumers and Brands

Taylor Royce

Copyright © 2024 Taylor Royce

All rights reserved.

DEDICATION

To individuals who view data as more than simply numbers and instead view it as a potent instrument for inspiring, connecting, and changing the marketing industry.

To the visionaries who work to create relationships based on authenticity and trust by bridging the gap between brands and consumers.

And to everyone who thinks that deliberate, data-driven tactics can generate significant innovation and change.

I'm dedicating this book to you.

CONTENTS

ACKNOWLEDGMENTS..1
DISCLAIMER..3
CHAPTER ONE..1
The Data Dilemma..1
    1.1 The Explosion of Data..1
    1.2 The Paradox of Marketing..4
    1.3 The Myth of the Consumer..6
    1.4 The Deficit in Trust..8

CHAPTER TWO...11
The Faulty Structure..11
    2.1 Power of Platform...11
    2.2 Privacy Aspects...13
    2.3 The Obstacle of Regulation..15
    2.4 The Advertising Coil...17

CHAPTER THREE..21
The Renaissance of Marketing...21
    3.1 Redefining the Goal of Marketing......................................21
    3.2 Fostering Confidence..23
    3.3 Focus on the Customer...25
    3.4 Ethics of Data..27

CHAPTER FOUR...32
Revolution in Lean Marketing..32
    4.1 Conventional Marketing's Inefficiency..............................32

4.2 The Mentality of Lean Marketing.. 34

4.3 Constructing a Lean Marketing Framework................................... 37

4.4 Assessing Achievement... 39

CHAPTER FIVE.. 43

The Framework for StoryBrands.. 43

5.1 Recognizing Your Clientele.. 43

5.2 Telling the Story of Your Brand... 46

5.3 Constructing a Sales Funnel... 48

5.4 Producing Captivating Material... 51

CHAPTER SIX.. 55

The 80/20 Principle... 55

6.1 Determining Areas with High Impact.. 55

6.2 Improving the Acquisition of Customers...................................... 58

6.3 Improving Client Retention.. 59

6.4 Making Use of Data for Development... 61

CHAPTER SEVEN... 64

Insights Driven by Data.. 64

7.1 Data Gathering and Administration... 64

7.2 Interpretation and Analysis of Data... 67

7.3 Analysis of Predictive Data.. 69

7.4 Information Display.. 71

CHAPTER EIGHT.. 75

Instruments and Technology.. 75

8.1 Automated Marketing... 75

8.2 Client Relationship Management (CRM)...................................... 78

8.3 The Intelligence (AI) component.. 80

8.4 Security and Privacy of Data... 82

CHAPTER NINE...**86**

A World Focused on the Customer...**86**

9.1 Individualization and Tailoring... 86

9.2 Practical Promotion.. 88

9.3 AI's Function.. 91

9.4 Ethical Points to Consider... 93

CHAPTER TEN... **96**

Constructing an Improved Future..**96**

10.1 Cooperation with Industry.. 96

10.2 Training and Education.. 99

10.3 Assessing Effect.. 101

10.4 An Appeal for Input.. 104

ABOUT THE AUTHOR..**108**

ACKNOWLEDGMENTS

My sincere thanks goes out to all the people and institutions who helped make this book possible.

First and foremost, I would like to express my sincere gratitude to my mentors and coworkers for kindly sharing their knowledge and wisdom. Your advice and support have been crucial in helping to shape our work.

We would especially want to thank the experts in research and marketing who shared their knowledge and practical experiences. Your suggestions have improved the book's substance and added useful viewpoints that raise its worth.

My editor and the publishing team have my sincere gratitude for their steadfast support and commitment. This book would not exist without your painstaking attention to detail and dedication to perfection.

I express my gratitude to my family and friends for their endurance, comprehension, and steadfast faith in me. Your encouragement and strength have been a continual source.

Lastly, I would like to express my gratitude to every reader who will interact with this book. This work is truly inspired by your quest for knowledge and enthusiasm for cutting-edge marketing strategies.

I appreciate all of your help and contributions.

DISCLAIMER

"Marketing in the Data Age: Linking Consumers and Brands" contains content that is solely meant to be used for general educational purposes. The author and publisher do not guarantee the correctness, reliability, or completeness of the material presented herein, even though every effort has been taken to assure its accuracy and completeness.

Based on current information and industry practices, the author's ideas and experiences are reflected in this book. The information presented here is not meant to be professional advice and should not be interpreted as such. It is recommended that readers obtain professional advice for any specific problems or queries pertaining to data analysis, marketing, or any other pertinent topic.

Liability for any actions made based on the information in this book is disclaimed by the author and publisher. By using this book, readers consent to release the publisher and author from all liability for losses or damages resulting from the use or misuse of the information included in it.

This book contains no trademarks or brand names that are not owned by their respective owners. Such trademarks or brand names are included here without any indication of support or connection.

It is recommended that readers use their own discretion and judgment while putting the ideas and methods covered in this book into reality.

CHAPTER ONE

The Data Dilemma

Data is being created at a rate that has never been seen before in the modern digital era. Data accessibility and availability have changed sectors and created new chances for expansion, creativity, and consumer interaction. Nonetheless, there are a lot of difficulties associated with this data explosion. Both organizations and consumers face challenges due to the overwhelming amount of data, the difficulties in managing it, and the moral dilemmas associated with its use. We examine the various aspects of the data issue in this chapter, going into the intricacies of the data explosion, the marketing paradox, the consumer dilemma, and the trust deficit.

1.1 The Explosion of Data

The amount of data generated worldwide is increasing at an exponential rate every second. The sources of data are numerous and diverse, ranging from sensor data from Internet of Things devices to social media interactions and online purchases. This phenomenon, which is sometimes called the "data explosion," affects people, governments, and corporations profoundly.

- **The Data Generation Scale:** The amount of data produced worldwide is astounding. Digital information is constantly expanding due to the billions of emails, social media posts, and online transactions that occur every day. The globe is predicted to produce 463 exabytes of data every day by 2025. Organizations face both benefits and drawbacks from this data flood. Even though it offers never-before-seen chances for creativity and insights, organizing and interpreting such enormous volumes of data is quite difficult.

- **The Difficulty of Data Administration:** The problem of efficiently managing the growing amount of data is here to stay. Concerns of data processing, retrieval, and storage must be addressed by organizations. The sheer amount and diversity of data often proves too much for traditional data management solutions to handle. In order to assist enterprises in managing the flood of data, new technologies including cloud computing, big data analytics, and artificial intelligence have been developed. These technologies do, however, present a unique set of difficulties, such as issues with scalability, pricing, and security.

- **Complexity and Variety of Data:** Variety is equally as important as volume in the data explosion. There are three different types of data: semi-structured, unstructured, and structured. Databases and other structured data are simple to organize and examine. On the other hand, unstructured data—like emails, posts on social media, and videos—is more challenging to handle and calls for sophisticated analytics methods in order to glean valuable insights. The extremely difficult process of data management is made even more onerous by the complexity of data.

1.2 The Paradox of Marketing

The relevance of data in marketing has increased along with its volume. More information is available to marketers than ever before, enabling them to create campaigns that are highly targeted and customized. But this wealth of data has also led to a paradox: data-driven marketing can be very successful, but it also runs the risk of upsetting customers and undermining their trust.

- **The Promise of Personalization:** With the use of data, marketers can give customers individualized experiences. Marketers are able to customize their messaging to the needs and interests of specific individuals by examining data on customer behavior, preferences, and demographics. This degree of customization has the potential to improve customer experiences, boost engagement, and boost loyalty. However, the quality and accuracy of the data as well as marketers' ability to appropriately analyze and apply it are what determine how effective personalization is.

- **The Danger of Excessive Personalization:** Personalization can improve consumer satisfaction, but there's a thin line separating helpfulness from intrusiveness. Consumers may become uneasy and lose trust if they see that they are being unduly watched or singled out due to excessive personalization. If customers believe their data is being exploited to influence them or violate their privacy, they can become cautious about sharing it. This paradox emphasizes the need for a data-driven marketing strategy that strikes a compromise between protecting customer privacy and providing tailored experiences.

- **Data Silos and Fragmentation:** The dispersion of data across numerous platforms and organizational departments is a problem for data-driven marketing. When several departments within a company gather and retain data separately, it creates data silos that result in inconsistent data and a fragmented customer view. Because of this fragmentation, marketing campaigns may be less successful and it may be more challenging to communicate with customers in a coherent and consistent manner.

1.3 The Myth of the Consumer

Today's consumers are better informed and more powerful than ever. They can study products, compare pricing, and read reviews before making a purchase since they have access to a wealth of information. But this wealth of information can also lead to overwhelm and misunderstanding, which is referred to as the "consumer conundrum."

- **Information Overload:** Consumers may find it difficult to process the vast amount of information available to them. The process of making decisions can get complicated and time-consuming, involving anything from product details and reviews to social media endorsements and price comparisons. Sifting through the clutter to get trustworthy information may be difficult for consumers, which could result in decision fatigue and annoyance.

- **Paradox of Choice:** The multitude of options at a consumer's disposal might result in the paradox of choice, which states that having too many options causes anxiety and makes decision-making more difficult. This may lead to consumers being unable to make a decision at all, feeling indecisive and dissatisfied with their selections, or even experiencing decision paralysis. Marketers need to resolve this dilemma by helping consumers make decisions more easily and by giving them information that is pertinent, clear, and succinct.

- **Protective Issues:** Privacy issues are becoming increasingly important as consumers become more conscious of how their data is gathered and utilized. At the center of the customer dilemma is the trade-off between privacy and convenience. Customers like tailored experiences and offers, but they are also growing more worried about the usage, storage, and sharing of their data. As a result, there is an increasing need for control, openness, and confidence in the way businesses handle customer data.

1.4 The Deficit in Trust

In the interaction between customers and businesses, trust is essential. But trust is becoming more and more brittle in the digital era. There is a rising lack of confidence between customers and enterprises as a result of data misuse, high-profile data breaches, and perceived openness.

- **The Consequences of Data Breach**: Publicly announced data breaches have reduced consumer confidence in an organization's ability to secure its data. Not only does the exposure of sensitive material negatively impact the individuals concerned, but it also harms the reputation of the responsible company. It is expensive to recover from a data breach in terms of monetary damages as well as the long-term effects on customer confidence.

- **Accountability and Transparency**: Transparency is now essential to establishing and preserving confidence in the face of mounting worries about data security and privacy. Customers want businesses to be open and honest about the ways in which their data is gathered, utilized, and distributed. This involves being transparent about data protection measures, consent procedures, and data policies. Accountability is also essential; businesses must accept accountability for protecting customer data and be ready to react quickly to any breaches or misuse.

- **Building Consumer Trust:** Proactive action is necessary to preserve and rebuild consumer trust. Prioritizing data security and privacy, putting strong data protection mechanisms in place, and promoting an accountable and transparent culture are all necessary for organizations. Rebuilding trust can be facilitated by being transparent with customers and giving them control over their data. Third-party certifications, regulatory compliance, and ethical data practices can all serve as additional evidence of an organization's dedication to safeguarding customer data.

The data problem is a complex issue that affects every

component of the contemporary business environment. Although the data explosion presents previously unheard-of benefits, it also complicates data management, marketing, consumer behavior, and trust issues. To effectively navigate this predicament, one must adopt a well-rounded strategy that takes advantage of data's power while tackling the moral, pragmatic, and strategic issues it raises.

CHAPTER TWO

THE FAULTY STRUCTURE

A complex web of issues has surfaced in the quickly changing digital landscape, exposing the flaws in our existing structures. What can be called a "broken system" is a result of a number of factors, including the dominance of large platforms, the growing worries about privacy, the difficulty of establishing regulations that work, and the overwhelming power of marketing. This chapter explores these important topics, including the influence that platforms wield, user privacy concerns, legislative obstacles that governments must overcome, and the unrelenting force of contemporary marketing.

2.1 Power of Platform

The emergence of digital platforms has brought about a transformation in the global economy, generating novel prospects for interconnectivity, trade, and creativity.

However, there are also serious worries about consumer choice, market fairness, and the impact on society due to the concentration of power among a small number of dominating platforms.

- **The Principal Platforms' Dominance:** A small number of platforms, like Google, Facebook, Amazon, and Apple, have unparalleled power in today's digital economy. These platforms act as entry points to a multitude of markets, communication avenues, and information sources. Because of their supremacy, they may control information access, affect customer behavior, and reshape the competitive environment. The possibility of monopolistic actions and market competition are called into doubt by this concentration of power.

- **Network Effects and Barriers to Entry:** The idea of network effects is one of the main elements influencing platform power. A self-reinforcing cycle occurs when more users join a platform, increasing its value and drawing in even more users. This makes it harder for new competitors to enter the market since it gets harder to compete with well-established platforms that have already reached a critical mass. The end effect is a market environment in which a small number of powerful firms can restrict customer choice and hinder innovation.

- **Information as a Basis of Strength**: The lifeblood of internet platforms is data. These platforms' massive data collection gives them insights into the trends, tastes, and behavior of its user base. Platforms may further solidify their supremacy by refining their algorithms, optimizing their services, and providing individualized experiences thanks to this data-driven edge. But this concentration of data also brings up issues with data security, privacy, and misuse potential.

2.2 Privacy Aspects

User privacy issues have increased in tandem with the strength of digital platforms. Customers, authorities, and privacy advocates are all very concerned about the gathering, storing, and use of personal data by these platforms.

- **The Extent of Data Collection:** Users' personal data is gathered by digital platforms in large quantities, frequently without their knowledge or consent. This information covers a wide range of topics, including social connections, browsing history, and geographical data. Due to the enormous amount and granularity of data being gathered, individuals might not completely understand how much of their personal information is being recorded and examined, which raises serious privacy concerns.

- **The Dangers of Misusing Data:** In the digital age, one of the biggest concerns is the possibility of personal data being misused. Among the hazards that users encounter include data breaches, unauthorized access, and the sale of personal information to third parties. In addition, a person may feel invaded and lose control over their own information if their personal data is used for targeted advertising and other commercial reasons. The lack of openness surrounding the methods platforms employ to gather, retain, and use data exacerbates these dangers.

- **Consumer Awareness and Trust**: As consumer skepticism and mistrust of digital platforms have grown, so too has awareness of privacy issues. A rising number of users are growing wary of disclosing personal information online, which is fueling demand for platforms to provide more openness, control, and accountability. But customers frequently feel exposed and helpless due to the complexity of privacy policies and the absence of intuitive, user-friendly tools for adjusting privacy settings.

2.3 The Obstacle of Regulation

Policymakers and governments face enormous hurdles in regulating the digital landscape. The worldwide reach of digital platforms, the swift rate of technology innovation, and the intricate interaction of market forces pose challenges to the establishment of regulations that are both effective and enforceable.

- **Technological Changes Pace:** The speed at which technology is developing is one of the main obstacles to digital platform regulation. The technology that regulations are intended to control may have evolved or changed by the time they are drafted, discussed, and put into action, making the restrictions antiquated or useless. As a result, regulations are always playing catch-up with new developments, leading to a never-ending cycle of catch-up.

- **Aspects of Jurisdiction and Enforcement:** Regulatory efforts are complicated by the worldwide character of internet platforms. Platforms frequently operate in several jurisdictions, each with its own legal framework. Because of this, platforms may be able to take advantage of legal gaps or relocate their operations to more permissive areas, making it more difficult to enforce restrictions. Furthermore, the absence of global agreement on digital governance makes the process of developing a logical and functional regulatory framework even more difficult.

- **Balancing Innovation and Regulation:** Protecting consumers and ensuring fair competition must coexist with the goal of promoting innovation and economic expansion, which is a challenging task for governments. Regulations that are too onerous can limit the advantages of digital technology, discourage investment, and inhibit innovation. Conversely, an absence of regulation may result in unfair business practices, invasions of privacy, and other unfavorable outcomes. For policymakers, striking the appropriate balance is a difficult and never-ending task.

2.4 The Advertising Coil

Though it has always been a potent instrument for shaping customer behavior, marketing has become an intricate and ubiquitous machine in the digital age. With the help of psychological manipulation, data-driven insights, and targeted advertising, marketing has become a powerful tool that not only shapes consumer choices but also social norms and values.

- **The Influence of Tailored Promotions:** Advertising has undergone a revolution because of digital platforms, which allow for highly targeted campaigns that deliver messages specifically to target consumers. The massive volumes of user data that are gathered enable advertisers to segment audiences according to demographics, behavior, and interests, enabling this degree of precision. Targeted advertising creates issues with privacy, manipulation, and potential exploitation even if it can be more effective and efficient than traditional techniques.

- **The Morality of Deception:** The distinction between manipulation and persuasion has become more hazy in marketing due to the use of data and psychology. Today, marketers may create messages that aim to elicit strong feelings from consumers, sway their decisions, and change their behavior by utilizing insights into human behavior and cognitive biases. Although this is a logical development of marketing strategies, it also raises moral concerns regarding the degree of consumer manipulation that occurs without the knowledge or agreement of the target audience.

- **The Impact on the Community**: The marketing machine influences society at large in addition to influencing the behavior of individual consumers. Marketing messages have the power to shape society norms, values, and expectations. They frequently encourage materialism, consumerism, and irrational notions of happiness and success. Because of the widespread reach of digital marketing and the ability of platforms to magnify certain messages, marketing has the potential to significantly influence social and cultural dynamics.

The consolidation of platform power, the degradation of privacy, the difficulties associated with regulation, and the ubiquitous effect of the marketing machine describe the dysfunctional structure of today's digital world. A holistic strategy that takes into account the intricate interactions between technology, legislation, ethics, and consumer behavior is needed to address these concerns. We cannot aspire to develop a digital ecosystem that is transparent, equitable, and respectful of people's rights and social values unless we first acknowledge and address these issues.

CHAPTER THREE

THE RENAISSANCE OF MARKETING

The field of marketing is going through a significant change that is sometimes called the "Marketing Renaissance." Conventional methods are being reassessed and reformulated in this new period to conform to the changing needs of society and consumers in terms of ethics. The main tenets of this renaissance are examined in this chapter, including reframing the goal of marketing, establishing trust, adopting consumer-centricity, and upholding data ethics. Every one of these components signifies a basic change in the way marketing is done, emphasizing the need for a strategy that is more accountable, open, and customer-focused.

3.1 Redefining the Goal of Marketing

Selling goods or services is no longer the exclusive goal of marketing. Its original goal has expanded to include sustainability, social responsibility, and the production of value that goes beyond financial gain. This newfound purpose is changing the way businesses interact with their customers and the part they play in society.

- **From Profit-Driven to Purpose-Driven:** The main goals of traditional marketing were to increase sales and profits. But in the modern market, people are looking more and more for companies that represent values beyond profit. These days, businesses must state their explicit goal in terms of social, environmental, or ethical objectives. The transition in marketing from profit-driven to purpose-driven is a reflection of the increasing understanding that companies have an obligation to make constructive contributions to society.

- **Corporate Social Responsibility (CSR):** A Role Corporate Social Responsibility, or CSR, is now a key component of contemporary marketing tactics. Companies are using corporate social responsibility (CSR) programs to show their support for causes like social justice, the environment, and community development. These programs not only improve a brand's reputation but also appeal to customers who give ethical factors first priority while making purchases. As a result, corporate social responsibility (CSR) is now an integral part of a brand's identity and marketing strategy rather than a side project.

- **Creating Shared Value:** By incorporating social and environmental concerns into the fundamental business plan, the idea of creating shared value (CSV) transcends typical corporate social responsibility (CSR). Businesses that adopt CSV aim to solve societal issues in methods that yield financial benefits. This strategy builds long-lasting relationships with customers, staff members, and other stakeholders who have similar values, in addition to strengthening the brand's purpose.

3.2 Fostering Confidence

In the current era of digital mistrust and information overload, developing trust has become a top issue for marketers. Any effective brand-consumer connection is built on trust, which is becoming more difficult to gain and simpler to lose in the current environment.

- **Openness as a Means of Establishing Trust:** Trust with customers must be established and maintained via transparency. Companies who are transparent about their supply chains, business procedures, and use of data have a higher chance of gaining the audience's trust. In order to be transparent, brands must communicate clearly, avoiding deceptive claims, giving accurate information, and owning up to their mistakes when they happen. Being transparent promotes honesty and dependability, two qualities that are essential for building trust.

- **Consistency and Authenticity:** Over time, consistent and genuine behavior fosters trust. Customers are adept at identifying discrepancies between a brand's stated intentions and its real actions. For instance, a company will rapidly lose credibility if it advocates for environmental sustainability but yet engages in environmentally harmful activities. In order to be considered authentic, businesses must adhere to their declared beliefs and goals, making sure that all facets of their business and communications support their main goals.

- **Social Proof's Function:** Trust is greatly aided by social proof, which includes client testimonials, reviews, and endorsements from influential people. Customers frequently base their decisions on what to buy on the advice and experiences of others. Good feedback and recommendations from reliable sources can increase a brand's legitimacy and dependability. But it's crucial that social proof is real; phony testimonials or false recommendations can backfire and cause mistrust.

3.3 Focus on the Customer

The core of the marketing renaissance is the trend towards consumer-centricity. Consumers of today demand meaningful interaction, tailored experiences, and brands that actually attend to their wants and requirements. Businesses that adopt a consumer-centric strategy must center all of their marketing initiatives around the needs of their target audience.

- **Personalization and Relevance:** In today's consumer-centric marketing, personalization is a vital component. Brands are able to customize their messaging, offers, and experiences to each individual consumer's unique requirements and preferences by utilizing data and insights. This degree of pertinence boosts marketing campaign efficacy in addition to augmenting customer happiness. Personalization needs to be done carefully though, maintaining personal space and avoiding coming out as invasive.

- **Activation and Interaction:** Active engagement and interaction are further aspects of consumer-centricity that go beyond personalization. More and more, brands are putting their energy into developing two-way channels of communication where customers can engage with the brand, offer feedback, and take part in brand-related activities. Increased brand loyalty and advocacy result from this interaction, which strengthens the bond between the customer and the company. Among the most important instruments for enabling this communication are social networking sites, channels for customer support, and discussion boards.

- **Compassion and Perception:** Empathy the capacity to comprehend and experience another person's emotions is the fundamental component of consumer-centricity. Companies that show empathy in their marketing communicate a sincere concern for the goals, struggles, and experiences of their target audience. This entails hearing what customers have to say, attending to their problems, and demonstrating a dedication to enhancing their lives via the brand's products. Deeper emotional connections are cultivated by empathic marketing, which has the potential to build enduring brand loyalty.

3.4 Ethics of Data

Data has developed into a potent tool for marketers in the

digital age, allowing for previously unheard-of degrees of personalisation and targeting. But this authority also carries the burden of using data in an ethical manner. As customers demand more accountability from organizations and grow more conscious of how their personal information is utilized, data ethics is becoming a crucial factor in the marketing renaissance.

- **Respect for Privacy:** A cornerstone of data ethics is upholding the privacy of consumers. Companies need to make sure that the way they gather, handle, and utilize personal information respects each person's right to privacy. This entails getting express consent before collecting data, being open and honest about data usage, and giving users choices about how their data is used. Legal foundations for ethical data practices have been established by privacy rules, such as the General Data Protection Regulation (GDPR) in Europe. However, for brands to truly respect privacy, compliance alone is not enough.

- **Avoiding Data Exploitation:** Another aspect of

ethical data use is avoiding using customer data for detrimental or manipulative objectives. This covers actions like selling data to third parties without permission, manipulating data to target individuals with predatory marketing, and exploiting data. Companies need to be aware of the possible drawbacks of their data practices and make sure that their use of data is improving the consumer experience rather than being exploitative.

- **Openness in the Use of Data:** Establishing trust in the use of data requires transparency. Customers need to know what information is being gathered, how it will be used, and who will have access to it. Companies should give consumers easy access to privacy policies, notify them on a regular basis of changes to data practices, and provide straightforward methods for them to adjust their data preferences. In addition to fostering trust, transparency in data usage gives customers the power to decide how best to engage with a brand.

- **Balancing Personalization and Privacy:** One of

the most important issues in data ethics is striking a balance between the requirement to preserve privacy and the desire for personalization. Although customers value tailored experiences, they are also worried about how much of their data is being utilized for this purpose. In order to make sure that personalization efforts are open, considerate, and in line with customer expectations, brands must carefully tread this delicate path. This could entail disclosing the advantages and disadvantages of personalization up front, limiting the usage of sensitive data, and offering obvious opt-in options.

The Marketing Renaissance signifies a significant change in the way brands view their interaction with society and consumers. Brands can succeed in this new era by reframing the goal of marketing, establishing trust, embracing consumer-centricity, and abiding by data ethics. While there are many obstacles to overcome, there are also many chances to build enduring relationships with customers, encourage steadfast devotion, and have a constructive impact on society. These guidelines will become crucial for every firm hoping to prosper in the twenty-first century as the marketing environment changes even more.

CHAPTER FOUR

Revolution in Lean Marketing

The increasing need for efficacy, efficiency, and agility in the marketing industry gave rise to the Lean Marketing Revolution. Lean concepts are being used to the reimagining of traditional marketing strategies, which are frequently hampered by inefficiencies and antiquated procedures. This chapter explores the shortcomings of conventional marketing, the adoption of a lean mentality, the creation of a lean marketing system, and the significance of success measurement. Organizations hoping to maximize their marketing tactics, cut costs, and produce more significant outcomes must have each of these elements.

4.1 Conventional Marketing's Inefficiency

Even though they worked well in the past, traditional marketing techniques are becoming less effective in the quick-changing digital world of today. These techniques frequently entail expensive expenses, drawn-out procedures, and a lack of flexibility, which can make it more difficult for brands to react swiftly to shifts in the market and customer demands.

- **High Costs and Low ROI:** Conventional marketing strategies frequently necessitate a substantial outlay of funds for media outlets including print, radio, and television. Although these campaigns might be expensive to create and launch, it is usually challenging to assess and maximize their return on investment (ROI). A significant amount of the marketing money may be squandered on tactics that fail to connect or successfully reach the target demographic due to the inability to correctly track performance.

- **Slow Adaptation to Market Changes:** Traditional marketing makes extensive use of carefully thought-out programs that are usually carried out over extended periods of time. It is challenging for companies to quickly adjust to changes in consumer behavior, new trends, or pressure from the competition because of this lack of adaptability. Therefore, by the time marketing initiatives are implemented, they can be out of current or irrelevant, which would result in lost opportunities and decreased efficacy.

- **Restricted Customer Feedback Loops:** Conventional marketing frequently uses a one-way communication approach in which companies push messages onto customers without getting back to them right away or with useful feedback. A brand's capacity to comprehend and address the wants, preferences, and concerns of its customers is hampered by this lack of in-the-moment engagement. Marketing initiatives are less likely to be in line with customer expectations in the absence of an effective feedback loop, which lowers engagement and satisfaction.

4.2 The Mentality of Lean Marketing

The core tenets of the lean marketing mindset are client

value, efficiency, and continual improvement. Organizations may streamline their marketing initiatives, cut down on waste, and develop more focused, successful campaigns by embracing this mentality.

- **Emphasize consumer Value:** Providing value to the consumer is the cornerstone of lean marketing. This implies that each and every marketing initiative must be well matched with the requirements and preferences of the intended market. Brands may make sure that their efforts are pertinent, interesting, and likely to produce favorable results like higher sales and customer loyalty by putting the value of their customers first.

- **Eliminating Waste:** The goal of lean marketing is to find and cut out any actions that don't benefit the client or advance the campaign's main objectives. This entails cutting back on pointless expenses, eliminating needless procedures, and optimizing workflows. Brands may allocate resources more effectively and make sure that every dollar spent on marketing has the greatest possible impact by getting rid of waste.

- **Continuous Improvement:** The dedication to ongoing improvement is a fundamental component of the lean marketing mindset. This entails routinely assessing marketing plans, techniques, and results to pinpoint areas in need of improvement. Organizations can improve their methods over time and create more effective and efficient marketing processes by cultivating a culture of ongoing learning and adaptation.

- **Agility and Flexibility:** Lean marketing places a strong emphasis on the value of these traits in adapting to shifting market conditions. This calls for a readiness to quickly change course, try out novel ideas, and modify campaigns in response to immediate feedback. Agile marketing teams are better able to adapt to changing market conditions, competitive landscapes, and consumer trends, ensuring that their work is impactful and relevant.

4.3 Constructing a Lean Marketing Framework

Organizations must create a lean marketing system that incorporates these ideas into every facet of their business operations in order to fully reap the benefits of the lean marketing philosophy. Adopting particular procedures, instruments, and practices that are intended to increase efficacy and efficiency is part of this system.

- **Interaction Across Functional Domains:** Interdepartmental and team collaboration is essential to the success of a lean marketing system. Instead of working independently from sales, product development, customer service, and other important departments, marketing should collaborate directly with them. Through cross-functional cooperation, marketing plans are informed by insights from many organizational departments and are in line with larger company objectives.

- **Decision Making Driven by Data:** An essential part of a lean marketing system is data. Organizations can obtain profound insights into consumer behavior, marketing performance, and market trends by utilizing data analytics. With the use of this information, marketers are better equipped to decide what to do, adjust their plans in the moment, and direct resources toward the most successful avenues and methods. The process of continuous improvement is aided by data-driven decision-making, which offers useful feedback on what is and is not working.

- **Iterative Campaign Development:** A lean marketing system prioritizes iterative development over large-scale, long-term campaigns. In order to do this, smaller, testing campaigns must be launched. Data must be gathered, and changes must be made before scaling up. Campaign development that is iterative lowers the possibility of failure, facilitates quick learning, and guarantees that marketing initiatives are continuously improved for better outcomes.

- **Lean Content generation:** A lean approach to

content generation can greatly increase efficiency. Content is a crucial component of contemporary marketing. This entails producing excellent content that can be reused, modularized, and adjusted for a variety of platforms and formats. Focusing on the material that connects with the audience the most is another aspect of lean content development, as opposed to creating a lot of information that has little significance or influence.

4.4 Assessing Achievement

Traditional metrics like impressions or clicks are not the only way to measure lean marketing performance. In order to give value to the client and meet corporate objectives, marketing initiatives must be evaluated using a thorough methodology.

- **KPIs, or key performance indicators:** KPIs that are carefully chosen and in line with the organization's objectives and customer value propositions are essential to lean marketing. These KPIs must be time-bound, relevant, measurable, achievable, and specific (SMART). Customer acquisition cost (CAC), customer lifetime value (CLV), conversion rates, and return on marketing investment (ROMI) are typical KPIs in lean marketing. Organizations can monitor the true effect of their marketing initiatives and make data-driven decisions for ongoing development by concentrating on these KPIs.

- **consumer Engagement and input:** In lean marketing, direct consumer input is a priceless metric. Companies should aggressively solicit feedback from their customers via questionnaires, testimonials, social media interactions, and other means. Customer feedback highlights opportunities for development and offers insights into how successfully marketing initiatives are connecting with the target demographic. High levels of interaction, like likes, comments, and return visits, also show how well marketing techniques work to establish enduring bonds with clients.

- **Measurability Agility:** Agile tracking and analysis

of performance is necessary for lean marketing measurement, which is not static. This entails routinely analyzing metrics, making necessary KPI adjustments, and being prepared to modify plans in response to current information. Agile measurement enables businesses to react swiftly to shifts in the consumer or market, preserving the efficacy and coherence of marketing initiatives.

- **Effect on Business Results:** Lean marketing effectiveness should ultimately be evaluated by looking at how it affects more general business results. This includes increasing sales, gaining market share, building a brand's reputation, and retaining customers. Lean marketing seeks to establish a clear connection between marketing initiatives and commercial achievement, guaranteeing that each endeavor advances the general well-being and expansion of the company.

The way businesses handle marketing has fundamentally changed as a result of the Lean Marketing Revolution. Businesses may overcome the inefficiencies of traditional marketing and create processes that are more responsive, effective, and in line with today's rapidly evolving marketplace by adopting the concepts of efficiency, agility, and customer value. Adopting lean marketing techniques will be crucial for companies looking to prosper in a dynamic and competitive environment as the marketing landscape continues to change.

CHAPTER FIVE

THE FRAMEWORK FOR STORYBRANDS

For companies trying to make sense of their marketing and establish a meaningful connection with their customers, the StoryBrand Framework is an effective tool. This framework, created by Donald Miller, makes use of storytelling principles to create engrossing brand narratives that connect with target audiences. The fundamental components of the StoryBrand Framework are examined in this chapter, including developing a sales funnel, knowing your target audience, telling your brand's narrative, and producing interesting content. Every one of these elements is essential to a company's ability to engage customers and successfully convey its value.

5.1 Recognizing Your Clientele

Gaining a comprehensive understanding of your customer is the first stage in the StoryBrand Framework. This entails delving deeper into your target audience's requirements, wants, problems, and aspirations in addition to providing basic demographic data. Developing a message that connects and inspires action starts with a thorough understanding of your target audience.

- **Determining the Issue with the Customer:** Any successful brand narrative starts with the customer's issue. This issue may be philosophical (a bigger idea or value at stake), emotional (how that obstacle makes them feel), or external (a specific challenge they experience). Clearly identifying and articulating these issues is crucial to building a genuine connection with your audience. Customers are more likely to engage and trust a business when they perceive it to be aware of their challenges.

- **Determining the Goals of the Customer:** Beyond issues, it's critical to comprehend the goals that your clients have for themselves. What are their desires, aspirations, and goals? You may position your business as a journey partner and assist people in reaching their goals by recognizing their aspirations and providing solutions that support them. This forges a strong emotional bond that transcends the features and advantages of the product.

- **Segmenting Your Audience:** Within a target market, there are differences amongst clients. You can more successfully adapt your messaging by segmenting your audience depending on certain characteristics, such as behavior, needs, or stage in the customer journey. Because every group could have various goals and pain issues, you should highlight different aspects of your brand story for each one.

- **Creating a Customer Persona:** Detailed customer personas help you visualize your understanding of the customer. These personas are made-up depictions of your ideal clients that are based on actual information and analysis. Data on aspirations, behavior patterns, pain areas, psychographics, and demographics should all be included. Your messaging and content production are guided by customer personas, which guarantee that your communications are consistently pertinent and focused.

5.2 Telling the Story of Your Brand

The next phase is to create a brand narrative that portrays your company as the hero's guide, assisting the consumer in overcoming obstacles and realizing their objectives, once you have a thorough understanding of them. Inspired by traditional storytelling concepts, the StoryBrand Framework provides a well-defined framework for this story.

- **The consumer as the Hero:** The consumer, not the brand, is the story's protagonist in the StoryBrand Framework. As a result, the emphasis is now on how the brand can support the customer's success rather than what it sells. The story revolves around the hero's journey, in which the brand assumes the role of the mentor who gives the hero the resources, counsel, and inspiration he or she needs to succeed.

- **Using Your Brand as a Reference Point:** Your

brand must exhibit authority and empathy in its role as the guide. Demonstrating empathy demonstrates your comprehension of the client's challenges and your sincere desire for their achievement. Authority makes your brand appear trustworthy and authoritative as a source of information. When empathy and authority are combined, trust is increased and clients are more likely to heed the advice of your brand.

- **Introducing the Plan:** A solid guide provides the hero with an easy-to-follow plan. This strategy, as described in the StoryBrand Framework, is an easy-to-implement procedure that guides the client from their issue to the intended result. It is important to simplify the plan by breaking it down into manageable phases that demonstrate that achievement is attainable.

- **Calling the Customer to Action:** A powerful call to action that nudges the customer to proceed is a feature of a captivating brand story. Whether the call to action is to make a purchase, subscribe to a newsletter, or schedule a consultation, it should be clear and precise. The intention is to instill a sense of urgency in the consumer and inspire them to follow the brand's instructions.

- **Talking About Success and Failure:** It's critical to emphasize both the possible negative effects of inaction (failure) and the positive effects of action (success) in order to give your brand story more complexity. Your message will have more emotional impact if you contrast what's at stake in a clear and concise manner. Customers should believe that acting will have undesirable effects, but adhering to your brand's instructions will have favorable, desired effects.

5.3 Constructing a Sales Funnel

Only when a brand story guides consumers through a sales funnel that turns curiosity into action can it be considered effective. According to the StoryBrand Framework, creating a sales funnel that seamlessly leads prospects from awareness to decision-making and, eventually, to purchase is crucial.

- **Awareness Stage:** The objective at this point in the sales funnel is to raise awareness of your company and its offerings. This is the point at which your brand story starts to captivate prospective clients by offering content that speaks to their issues and goals. At this point, the content should be instructive, informative, and attention-grabbing without being unduly commercial.

- **Deliberation Stage:** Following brand awareness, consumers proceed to the deliberation stage, where they assess various options and remedies. In this case, your brand narrative should emphasize establishing credibility and proving value. Case studies, endorsements, thorough product descriptions, and comparisons that accentuate the special advantages of your brand will help you accomplish this.

- **Decision Stage:** Customers are prepared to decide what to buy at this point. At this point, your marketing and content should clearly state the benefits of your brand and include calls to action. Guarantees, discounts, and offers can all be useful in persuading clients to complete the transaction.

- **Retention and Advocacy:** After a transaction, the sales funnel continues. Maintaining a customer base and converting them into brand ambassadors is essential for sustained success. Customer support, loyalty programs, and follow-up emails are examples of post-purchase engagement that helps keep the connection going. Content consumers are more likely to become loyal supporters of your business and refer it to others, therefore extending your reach naturally.

- **Automation and Optimization:** You should think about automating important steps in the process to make sure your sales funnel runs well. Based on their behavior and funnel stage, marketing automation solutions can assist in providing the right information to the right customer at the right moment. Maintaining and improving your sales funnel on a regular basis is also crucial. To increase conversion rates, this entails examining performance indicators, locating bottlenecks, and implementing fixes.

5.4 Producing Captivating Material

A compelling story is the StoryBrand Framework's vitality. It serves as the engine that drives your sales funnel and conveys your brand's narrative. The secret to increasing client engagement and accomplishing your marketing objectives is producing content that enthralls, informs, and inspires your audience.

- **Information that Speaks to the Hero's Journey:** Each and every content you produce needs to be connected to the hero's journey of your customers. Whether it's an email, blog post, video, or social media update, the material should address the issues the consumer is facing, provide advice, and reaffirm the strategy you outlined in your brand story. You can guarantee that your material will always be compelling and current by regularly matching it to the hero's path.

- **Multichannel Content Approach:** Consumers engage with companies via a variety of platforms, and the diversity of these interactions should be reflected in your content strategy. Create material that can be shared on a variety of channels, such as your website, social media accounts, email newsletters, and more. Make sure that your material is appropriate for the structure and context of each platform as different channels have different strengths and audience preferences.

- **Storytelling Methods for Producing Content:** An engaging piece of content is centered around storytelling. To make your material more engaging, use narrative strategies including emotional appeal, conflict and resolution, and relatable characters. Not only can storytelling hold an audience's interest, but it also makes difficult concepts simple enough for them to understand and retain.

- **Visual and Interactive material:** In the current

digital environment, the significance of visual and interactive material is growing. Multimedia content like infographics, interactive tests, and videos can increase interaction and give your brand a more engaging narrative. Interactive content promotes greater engagement and connection with your audience, while visual material is especially good at swiftly and vividly conveying information.

- **Consistency and Frequency:** Sustaining client involvement requires consistency. Regular content creation helps develop a devoted following and maintains your business at the forefront of consumers' minds. It's crucial to strike a balance between frequency and quality, though. Rather from overwhelming your readers with quantity, concentrate on continuously producing high-quality content. You can maintain this balance and meet your content objectives by using a content calendar.

- **Determining the Effectiveness of Content:** Measuring the efficacy of your material is crucial to optimizing its impact. Keep an eye on important indicators like social shares, engagement rates, click-through rates, and conversion rates to determine what appeals to and repels from your audience. Make use of these insights to hone your content strategy, concentrating on the kinds of material that yield the greatest outcomes.

A methodical strategy for refining your brand message and making a meaningful connection with consumers is provided by the StoryBrand Framework. You may increase consumer engagement and accomplish your marketing goals by getting to know your target audience, developing a strong brand narrative, constructing a successful sales funnel, and producing interesting content. The StoryBrand Framework's tenets continue to be an effective tool for businesses trying to stand out and leave a lasting impression, even as the marketing landscape changes.

CHAPTER SIX

The 80/20 Principle

The Pareto Principle, sometimes referred to as the 80/20 Principle, is a potent idea in marketing and business that says that 80% of results are frequently the result of 20% of causes. According to this theory, the majority of results in marketing are usually driven by a tiny amount of efforts or resources. By concentrating on high-impact areas that substantially contribute to corporate growth, more effective strategies may be achieved by comprehending and putting the 80/20 Principle into practice. This chapter explores the application of the 80/20 Principle to business, including how to pinpoint high-impact areas, maximize client acquisition, improve customer retention, and use data to drive corporate expansion.

6.1 Determining Areas with High Impact

The initial phase of implementing the 80/20 Principle

involves pinpointing the high-impact domains inside your enterprise—those crucial elements that yield the most noteworthy outcomes. Businesses can increase their efficacy and efficiency by focusing their resources in these areas.

- **Revenue Stream Analysis:** To begin, examine your income sources to ascertain which goods, services, or clientele groups are most important to your overall profitability. It is normal to discover that the majority of revenue is generated by a tiny number of consumers or items. You can more efficiently allocate resources by concentrating on these high-impact regions, making sure that your marketing initiatives are in line with the most lucrative prospects.

- **Evaluating Marketing Channels:** The return on investment (ROI) from various marketing channels varies. Determine which channels are bringing in the most customers, leads, and sales. For instance, you can discover that 80% of your leads are produced by 20% of your advertising budget. It is possible to maximize your marketing budget and receive better results with less work by concentrating on these high-performing channels.

- **Prioritizing client Segments:** There are probably more valuable segments within your client base than others. These could be repeat buyers, clients with larger average order values, or customers that recommend business more frequently. Your marketing efforts can increase customer satisfaction and lifetime value by giving priority to these areas.

- **Identifying Key Products or Services:** In a similar vein, certain goods or services might influence your success in an excessively large way. Determine which products are the most well-liked or have the largest profit margins, then concentrate on enhancing and advertising them. Reorganizing your product or service portfolio to highlight these high-impact areas can boost revenue and foster a sense of brand loyalty.

6.2 Improving the Acquisition of Customers

A key component of business growth is customer acquisition, and using the 80/20 Principle in this process will help you concentrate on the most successful methods of drawing in new clients.

- **Targeted Advertising:** Utilize data to pinpoint the 20% of channels and demographics that produce the most results for your advertising spend, as opposed to distributing it over numerous platforms and audiences. Focusing only on these high-impact areas will help you cut expenses while generating more and better quality leads.

- **Accelerated Value Proposition Refinement:** Your value proposition should make it apparent what special advantages your company provides. You may improve your value offer by focusing on the elements that encourage the greatest number of conversions by examining which messages your target audience responds to the most. Pay attention to the 20% of messages that elicit 80% of the interest from customers.

- **Streamlining the Sales Funnel:** To reduce drop-offs and increase conversions, the sales funnel should be optimized. Examine your funnel to see which phases or points of contact influence a lead's likelihood of becoming a customer the most. You can dramatically raise your conversion rate by optimizing these crucial areas, such making your call-to-action more clear or decreasing friction in the checkout process.

- **Using Referral Programs:** Getting new consumers through referrals is frequently one of the most effective marketing strategies. You can increase the effectiveness of your referral program and attract new customers at a lower cost by identifying and rewarding the top 20% of your clientele who are most likely to recommend you to others.

6.3 Improving Client Retention

If anything, customer retention is even more crucial than

acquisition. Here, the 80/20 Principle can be used to concentrate on the tactics that generate the greatest repeat business for the business.

- **Putting the Emphasis on High-Value Clients:** Determine which 20% of your clientele are most important to your bottom line. Your retention efforts should be concentrated on these high-value clients. Provide customers with individualized experiences, special discounts, and first-rate customer support to win their loyalty.

- **Improving Customer Experience:** Examine client input to determine the main variables affecting client retention and satisfaction. Customer loyalty can frequently be disproportionately affected by a small number of crucial touchpoints, such as delivery timeliness, customer service contacts, or product quality. Enhancing these high-impact areas will help you greatly increase retention rates.

- **Creating Loyalty Programs:** Promoting recurring business can be accomplished through the use of loyalty programs. Pay attention to the 20% of incentives or bonuses that bring in 80% of your clients' engagement. This can entail exclusive savings, first dibs on brand-new items, or tailored deals predicated on past purchases.

- **Decreasing Churn:** Determine the primary causes of customer churn and take proactive measures to address these issues in order to reduce customer churn. The majority of churn is frequently caused by a small number of issues, such as subpar customer service or low engagement. You can lower attrition and increase client retention by concentrating on these crucial areas.

6.4 Making Use of Data for Development

An essential resource for successfully implementing the 80/20 Principle is data. Businesses can use data to their advantage by understanding which areas have the biggest effects on growth and tailoring their plans accordingly.

- **Decision Making Driven by Data:** Utilize data

analytics to determine which 20% of your components account for 80% of your outcomes. Key performance indicators (KPIs) pertaining to customer satisfaction, sales, marketing, and operational efficiency may fall under this category. Concentrating on these high-impact indicators can help you make better decisions that will propel your business forward.

- **Predictive Analytics:** By helping you foresee future trends and consumer behavior, predictive analytics frees up your time to concentrate on the areas that will most likely have the biggest effects on your company. One way to customize marketing efforts is to determine the customers who are most likely to make repeat purchases so that you may promote further interaction.

- **Automating High-Impact Processes:** By concentrating on the most significant procedures, automation can assist you in growing your company. When it is feasible, automate the 20% of jobs that require the greatest amount of time and resources but yield the greatest returns. This can entail data analysis, marketing efforts, and customer communications automation.

- **Continual Improvement:** In conclusion, the 80/20 Principle ought to be implemented as a continual process of development. Review your data frequently in order to spot new high-impact areas and modify your plans as necessary. You can make sure that your company stays competitive and adaptable in a market that is changing quickly by continuously honing in on your core competencies.

A useful technique for maximizing corporate and marketing strategy is the 80/20 Principle. Businesses may do more with less work by recognizing and concentrating on high-impact areas, improving customer acquisition, boosting customer retention, and utilizing data for growth. This strategy ensures long-term success in a cutthroat market by promoting sustainable growth in addition to efficiency gains.

CHAPTER SEVEN

INSIGHTS DRIVEN BY DATA

Data is becoming the most important resource for successful firms in the current digital era. Organizations may effectively satisfy consumer needs by optimizing processes, making informed decisions, and customizing strategies with the use of data-driven insights. The essential elements of using data to drive corporate success are examined in this chapter, with particular attention paid to data administration and collection, data analysis and interpretation, predictive analytics, and data visualization. Through comprehension and utilization of these components, enterprises can unleash the complete capability of their data to propel expansion and novelty.

7.1 Data Gathering and Administration

Efficient data collection and administration are the cornerstones of data-driven insights. The capacity to obtain significant insights is severely constrained in the absence of precise, pertinent, and orderly data. In order to guarantee that data is a trustworthy resource for decision-making, this section explores the procedures and best practices for data collection and management.

- **Determining Useful Information Sources:** Finding the data sources that are most pertinent to your company's goals is the first stage in the data collection process. These sources might be external, like social media platforms, market research, and industry studies, or internal, such as customer databases, sales records, and operational logs. Your data gathering efforts can be made more efficient and targeted by concentrating on data that directly affects your key performance indicators (KPIs).

- **Implementing Data Collection Tools:** The next stage is to implement the technologies and tools needed to collect data after the pertinent data sources have been located. IoT devices, website analytics tools, CRM systems, and diverse APIs that enable the integration of data from several platforms can all fall under this category. Selecting technologies that guarantee data consistency and quality while also capturing it effectively is essential.

- **Maintaining Data Quality:** The dependability of insights obtained from data depends critically on its quality. Regular cleansing and validation of data is necessary for data quality management in order to eliminate errors, duplication, and inconsistencies. Maintaining good data quality over time is facilitated by the establishment of explicit data governance standards, which include standardized data entry procedures and frequent audits.

- **Data Storage and Security:** Effective and safe storage solutions are another aspect of proper data management. It is imperative for businesses to select storage solutions that align with their data volume and access requirements, be it cloud storage, on-site servers, or a hybrid setup. To further safeguard sensitive data against breaches and unauthorized access, strong data security measures such as encryption, access limits, and frequent security assessments are necessary.

7.2 Interpretation and Analysis of Data

Gathering and organizing data is just the first step. Once raw data is analyzed and interpreted, it becomes truly valuable information that can be put to use. This section examines the methods and strategies applied to data analysis in order to produce insightful findings.

- **Choosing Proper Analytical Techniques:** Different analytical techniques are needed for different kinds of data. For instance, statistical methods may work well for analyzing quantitative data, whereas theme analysis may be necessary for qualitative data. Finding patterns, trends, and correlations in the data requires careful method selection. Complex datasets can be analyzed using methods like cluster analysis, regression analysis, and time-series analysis.

- **Contextualizing Data Insights:** The larger corporate environment needs to be taken into consideration when contextualizing data analysis.

This entails taking into account outside variables that could affect the data, such as competitive landscape, market trends, and economic situations. Businesses may make sure that their decisions are not only data-driven but also strategically aligned with their objectives by contextualizing findings.

- **Determining Crucial Measures:** Finding the critical KPIs in the analytical process that are most important to your business goals is crucial. These measurements, often known as KPIs, give a clear picture of performance and areas that need work. Businesses can successfully prioritize their efforts by concentrating on the 20% of measures that drive 80% of outcomes (aligning with the 80/20 Principle).

- **Avoiding Common Pitfalls:** Confirmation bias is a common mistake in data analysis, when analysts may inadvertently look for data to validate their preconceived notions. Instead of fitting the data to preconceived preconceptions, it is crucial to approach data analysis with an open mind and let the data drive conclusions. Furthermore, a sufficient and representative sample size is essential to the analysis's validity.

7.3 Analysis of Predictive Data

A potent technology that uses past data to predict future events is predictive analytics. Businesses can make proactive decisions by using statistical algorithms and machine learning approaches to predict trends, behaviors, and possible difficulties.

- **Understanding Predictive Models:** Predictive models make predictions about the future by analyzing past data to find patterns and relationships. Neural networks, decision trees, and regression models are examples of common prediction models. Every model has advantages and disadvantages, and the best option is determined by the precise prediction objectives, the properties of the data, and the necessary degree of accuracy.

- **Implementing Machine Learning**: By continuously

learning from new data and increasing forecast accuracy over time, machine learning is essential to predictive analytics. Large volumes of data can be analyzed using machine learning algorithms, which can spot minute patterns that conventional analytic techniques might overlook. Predictive analytics frequently uses methods like reinforcement learning, supervised learning, and unsupervised learning to improve decision-making.

- **Projecting Business Results:** Predictive analytics may be used in a number of business domains, including risk management, customer behavior forecasting, and sales forecasting. Businesses can predict future sales trends, for instance, by studying historical sales data. This information enables them to better plan marketing campaigns, manage pricing tactics, and modify inventory levels. Predictive analytics can also assist in identifying clients who are likely to leave, allowing for more focused retention tactics.

- **Difficulties and Points to Remember:** Predictive

analytics has many benefits, but there are drawbacks as well. Since erroneous or insufficient data might result in incorrect predictions, data quality and completeness are crucial. Predictive models also need to be updated frequently to account for modifications in consumer behavior and market conditions. Predictive analytics has ethical ramifications that should be taken into account as well, especially when it comes to issues like data bias and privacy.

7.4 Information Display

The last phase in the process of gaining data-driven insights is data visualization, which converts intricate data analysis into aesthetically appealing representations that stakeholders can quickly comprehend and act upon.

Selecting Appropriate Visualization Instruments: For data visualization, a variety of tools are available, each with unique advantages. Interactive dashboards and reports may be created with tools like Tableau, Power BI, and Google Data Studio, and they can be tailored to the requirements of various users. The complexity of the data, the amount of interaction necessary, and the particular visualization requirements of the business should all be taken into consideration when selecting a tool.

- **Creating Powerful Visualizations:** A data visualization's efficacy is determined by how well it can succinctly and effectively convey ideas. This entails choosing the right kind of graph or chart for the data, such as scatter plots for correlations, line charts for trends, or bar charts for comparisons. The most significant ideas should be highlighted in visualizations, and the viewer's attention should be deliberately directed by the use of color, size, and placement.

- **Narrating a Story Driven by Data:** Data visualization is a storytelling tool that goes beyond simple data presentation. Through the logical organization of visualizations, firms may produce a story that highlights critical insights and facilitates decision-making. This could entail presenting a broad overview first, then delving into more specific information, or it could entail showcasing trends throughout time to demonstrate how the company is changing.

- **Maintaining Usability and Accessibility:** Regardless of a stakeholder's level of technical proficiency, visualizations ought to be usable and accessible to everybody. This entails creating visualizations with labels, legends, and explanations that are simple to read and comprehend. Drill-downs and filters are examples of interactive features that can improve usability by letting users examine the data in greater detail.

In the current business environment, the capacity to extract insights from data is a vital competitive advantage. Businesses can use data to inform decisions, refine strategies, and eventually produce better results by concentrating on data collection and management, analysis and interpretation, predictive analytics, and visualization. Data-driven insights help organizations remain ahead of the curve and prosper in a world that is becoming more and more data-centric by helping them shape the future rather than just comprehending the past.

CHAPTER EIGHT

INSTRUMENTS AND TECHNOLOGY

In today's dynamic corporate environment, tools and technology are essential for increasing productivity, improving client interaction, and safeguarding information. This chapter explores the key technologies—marketing automation, customer relationship management (CRM) systems, artificial intelligence (AI), data privacy and security, and more that are revolutionizing marketing and CRM. All these elements are necessary for companies who want to compete in today's digitally-driven market.

8.1 Automated Marketing

Marketing automation has completely changed how companies interact with their clientele by enabling large-scale, efficient, and customized marketing campaigns. Businesses can ensure timely and consistent communication with their audience while concentrating on strategy and innovation by automating tedious chores and processes.

- **Streamlining Marketing Processes:** Email campaigns, social media posts, lead creation, and customer segmentation are just a few of the marketing tasks that marketing automation technologies can automate. Businesses may guarantee timely and consistent marketing efforts by automating these operations, freeing up valuable resources to concentrate on other strategic objectives.

- **Personalization at Scale:** Among the biggest benefits of marketing automation is the capacity to reach a broad audience with tailored content. Automation technologies may provide customized marketing communications that speak to specific consumers by utilizing customer data, which raises engagement and conversion rates. Automated email marketing, for instance, can be tailored to the preferences, purchase history, and behavior of the recipient, increasing open and click-through rates.

- **Lead Nurturing and Scoring:** Another important function of marketing automation is lead nurturing and scoring. Automation solutions can determine where a lead is in the purchasing process and provide pertinent information that advances them toward a purchase decision by monitoring and evaluating customer interactions. Lead scoring systems can also rank leads according to how likely they are to convert, allowing sales teams to concentrate their efforts on the most promising customers.

- **Measuring Campaign Effectiveness:** Marketing automation platforms offer comprehensive reporting and analytics tools that let companies assess a campaign's efficacy in real time. Companies can obtain significant insights into their operations by monitoring critical indicators like open rates, click-through rates, and conversion rates. Better outcomes are possible through ongoing optimization of marketing efforts thanks to this data-driven strategy.

8.2 Client Relationship Management (CRM)

The foundation of every customer-centric business strategy is provided by customer relationship management (CRM) solutions. These platforms offer a consolidated location for tracking sales, managing customer contacts, and analyzing customer data, all of which contribute to better company outcomes and greater customer connections.

- **Centralizing Customer Data:** By consolidating all customer-related data into a single location, a CRM system facilitates easy access to pertinent departments, such as customer assistance and sales and marketing. By ensuring that everyone in the company has a comprehensive and current understanding of every customer, this centralized approach enables more consistent and informed interactions.

- **Improving Customer Engagement**: By facilitating more timely and tailored contact, CRM systems assist companies in forging closer bonds with their clientele. CRM software lets organizations personalize their offers and communications to each customer based on their unique requirements and preferences by tracking consumer interactions across numerous touchpoints. This customized strategy increases client happiness and fosters retention and loyalty.

- **Improving Sales Productivity:** CRM systems give sales teams the resources they need to identify prospects, handle leads, and close deals faster. Sales teams can focus on high-value tasks, optimize workflows, and prioritize their efforts with the help of features like pipeline management, forecasting, and sales automation. CRM platforms also frequently interface with other tools, such e-commerce platforms and marketing automation, making the user experience easy for both sales teams and customers.

- **Analyzing Customer Behavior:** CRM systems provide firms with strong analytics tools that let them learn more about the preferences and behavior of their customers. Through the examination of information such as past purchases, client feedback, and interaction patterns, businesses can spot patterns and chances for expansion. By using a data-driven strategy, firms may enhance customer experiences, boost revenue, and make better decisions.

8.3 The Intelligence (AI) component

Artificial intelligence (AI) is radically changing how companies run by providing new avenues for creativity, productivity, and client interaction. Artificial intelligence (AI) is being utilized in marketing and customer relationship management to improve decision-making, automate complicated operations, and provide more individualized experiences.

- **Automating Complex processes:** Artificial intelligence (AI)-enabled solutions may automate labor-intensive, complex processes that would otherwise need a lot of human labor. AI, for instance, can be used to examine big databases, spot trends, and produce insights that guide marketing plans. AI-driven chatbots may also respond to consumer enquiries instantly, offering prompt assistance and freeing up human agents to work on more complicated problems.

- **Improving Decision-Making:** AI offers predictive analytics and deeper insights to help firms make more informed decisions. AI is able to recognize patterns in past data, predict future events, and suggest actions that maximize efficiency. AI, for example, may forecast consumer behavior, such as the chance of a purchase or churn, enabling companies to take proactive steps to increase sales or retain consumers.

- **Delivering Personalized Experiences:** AI is essential to providing large-scale, highly customized experiences. AI can generate dynamic content and offers that are customized to each individual's tastes by evaluating customer data, which will increase engagement and conversion rates. AI systems, for instance, might make product recommendations based on browsing patterns or previous purchases, giving customers a more relevant and pleasurable shopping experience.

- **Optimizing Marketing Spend:** By determining the most efficient channels, messaging, and tactics, AI may also assist companies in optimizing their marketing budgets. AI is able to make real-time campaign adjustments by continuously assessing performance data. This allows it to allocate resources to the most effective projects while cutting down on waste. With the use of this data-driven strategy, marketing budgets are utilized more effectively, increasing return on investment (ROI).

8.4 Security and Privacy of Data

Data protection is more crucial than ever in a time when it is a valuable asset. In addition to being required by law, data security and privacy are crucial for gaining and retaining client trust. The main factors and recommended procedures for data protection in the digital age are examined in this section.

- **Knowing About Data Privacy Laws:** A crucial component of data management is adhering to data privacy laws. Strict guidelines on the collection, storage, and use of personal data by corporations are enforced by laws like the California Consumer Privacy Act (CCPA) in the US and the General Data Protection Regulation (GDPR) in Europe. Companies need to make sure they are in complete compliance with these requirements, which includes getting consumers' express consent before collecting their data and giving them clear information about how the data will be used.

- **Implementing Robust Security Measures:** Robust security measures are necessary to safeguard consumer data against breaches and unauthorized access. This entails employing multi-factor authentication (MFA) to safeguard system access, putting encryption mechanisms in place to protect data both in transit and at rest, and routinely updating software to guard against security flaws. To find and fix any vulnerabilities, companies should also perform frequent penetration tests and security audits.

- **Training Staff on Data Security:** In data security, human mistake is frequently the weakest link. Employee training on data security best practices, such as identifying phishing attempts, creating strong passwords, and handling sensitive data securely, is therefore essential. Frequent training and awareness initiatives can greatly lower the chance of employee errors or carelessness leading to data breaches.

- **Building Customer Trust:** Customer trust is a direct result of data security and privacy. Strong customer connections are more likely to be developed and maintained by companies that place a high priority on data protection and are open and honest about their procedures. This entails giving clients control over their data, outlining explicit privacy standards, and responding quickly to any security incidents or data breaches. Establishing a commitment to safeguarding customer data allows firms to stand out in a crowded market and cultivate enduring customer loyalty.

The success of modern marketing and customer relationship management is largely dependent on technology and tools. Businesses may increase productivity, personalize consumer interactions, and foster trust in an increasingly digital world by utilizing marketing automation, CRM systems, artificial intelligence, and placing a high priority on data protection and security. Remaining ahead of the curve when it comes to technology will become crucial for companies looking to expand steadily and keep a competitive advantage.

CHAPTER NINE

A World Focused on the Customer

The move to a customer-first strategy is not simply a trend, but a need in today's cutthroat industry. Companies that put the needs, tastes, and experiences of their customers first succeed. This chapter explores the essential components of building a world where the consumer comes first, such as experience marketing, artificial intelligence (AI), personalization and customization, and the moral requirements that must underpin these actions.

9.1 Individualization and Tailoring

Customization and personalization are becoming essential components of contemporary consumer experiences. These procedures are necessary to build loyalty and lasting connections in a world where the client always comes first.

- **Knowing consumer Preferences:** Knowing

consumer preferences is the first step towards personalization. This entails gathering and examining information on consumer preferences, past purchases, and behavior. Businesses can use this data to customize their products and services to each customer's unique requirements and preferences, giving them a sense of value and understanding.

- **Customized Content and Offers:** Companies are able to develop customized content and offers after they have a firm grasp on the preferences of their clients. This could involve tailored marketing, product recommendations, or email campaigns. To increase the chance of a sale, an online merchant could utilize data analytics to suggest products based on a customer's past purchases or browsing behavior.

- **Product and Service Customization:** Customization goes beyond personalization by giving clients full control over the goods and services they get. This could include making complete custom solutions for specific clients or altering a product's attributes, like choosing the color or size. Customers that feel empowered by customization take an active role in their purchases, which can greatly increase customer happiness and loyalty.

- **The Effect on Client Loyalty:** Customization and personalization help to foster a strong sense of consumer loyalty. Customers are more inclined to come back to a company when they believe it understands and meets their specific demands. In crowded marketplaces, this loyalty can provide a substantial competitive advantage by increasing client lifetime value.

9.2 Practical Promotion

The emphasis in today's customer-first market has evolved from just making sales to making memorable experiences that connect with clients deeper. Experience marketing is about interacting with consumers in ways that go beyond conventional advertising and leaving a mark that encourages repeat business.

- **Creating Immersive Experiences:** Creating immersive experiences that arouse feelings and grab the attention of customers is experience marketing. This might be accomplished through immersive retail spaces, interactive events, or digital experiences like augmented reality and virtual reality (VR and AR). A VR experience that lets clients virtually try on makeup before making a purchase, for instance, might be offered by a cosmetics firm. This would be a novel and interesting method for customers to interact with the brand.

- **Narrative Techniques and Brand Storytelling:** The craft of narrative is essential to experience marketing. Strong emotional connections are more likely to be formed by brands that are able to deliver captivating stories that connect with their audience. Customers should be able to relate to the brand's identity through these tales, which should represent the company's values and mission. For instance, to attract clients that respect environmental responsibility, a sustainable fashion firm may tell tales of how their items are sourced responsibly.

- **Engaging All Senses:** To produce a more memorable experience, experiential marketing frequently incorporates a variety of senses. This could involve using aroma, sound, and pictures to create an atmosphere that people will remember. For example, retailers may employ particular music or fragrances in their establishments to improve the shopping experience and foster a closer emotional bond with their clientele.

- **Evaluating Experience Marketing's Impact:** Numerous measures, including social media engagement, brand memory, and consumer happiness, can be used to gauge the effectiveness of experience marketing. Businesses can evaluate the success of their experience campaigns and make the required improvements to improve subsequent efforts by monitoring these KPIs.

9.3 AI's Function

The way businesses connect with their clients is being revolutionized by Artificial Intelligence (AI). AI is essential for increasing personalization, boosting customer service, and optimizing marketing tactics in a world where the consumer comes first.

- **Improving Customization:** Artificial Intelligence makes possible a degree of customization that was not possible before. AI systems are able to forecast client behavior and find patterns in massive amounts of data, which enables businesses to provide highly tailored experiences. AI, for instance, can fuel recommendation engines, which provide more individualized experiences by making product or content recommendations based on a customer's previous interactions.

- **Improving Customer Service:** Chatbots and virtual assistants driven by AI are becoming more and more prevalent in customer support. These tools work around the clock and are able to respond to common questions, offer immediate assistance, and even help with complicated problems. AI improves customer service's overall effectiveness and responsiveness by freeing up human agents to concentrate on more difficult jobs.

- **Optimizing Marketing Strategies:** AI plays a key role in this process as well. AI may assist companies in determining the best marketing channels, customizing messages for target audiences, and even automating campaign management by evaluating data from several sources. By doing this, marketing campaigns become more effective and customers are guaranteed to receive timely and pertinent communications.

- **Customer insights and predictive analytics:** Predictive analytics is one of the most effective uses of AI. AI is able to forecast future consumer behavior by evaluating past data, including product purchases and potential churn times. This makes it possible for companies to act proactively to keep clients and increase revenue.

9.4 Ethical Points to Consider

The transition to a customer-first strategy has numerous advantages, but it also poses significant ethical questions. Companies that want to keep their connections with customers based on honesty and trust must carefully manage these difficulties.

- **Data Privacy and Consent:** It's critical for organizations to prioritize data privacy and secure explicit customer consent as they gather more data to support AI-driven insights and personalization. Clients must be given the choice to opt out and be informed about how their data will be handled. Ignoring data privacy can have serious negative effects on one's reputation and even result in legal repercussions.

- **Avoiding Manipulative Practices:** Experience marketing and personalization are useful tools, but they must be handled carefully. Companies should refrain from deceptive tactics that take advantage of consumer weaknesses or inflate the urgency of a situation. In order to protect consumers' confidence, ethical marketing entails being open and truthful with them.

- **Synergizing Automation with Human Touch:** Although automation and artificial intelligence have numerous benefits, they shouldn't completely replace human interaction. Consumers still appreciate face-to-face communication, particularly in delicate or complicated circumstances. Companies should make an effort to strike a balance between automation and human contact so that clients feel respected and heard.

- **Promoting Inclusivity and Diversity:** Diversity and inclusivity in marketing are also subject to ethical considerations. Companies need to make sure that the varied experiences and backgrounds of their clients are reflected in their marketing campaigns. This entails speaking inclusively, portraying a range of groups in promotional materials, and staying away from stereotypes.

- **Maintaining Availability:** In an era where customers come first, accessibility is a crucial moral factor. Companies need to make sure that all of their clients, including people with disabilities, can access their digital experiences, goods, and services. This shows a dedication to inclusion and social responsibility while also expanding the client base.

More than merely implementing new marketing techniques or technology are needed to create a customer-first world; a fundamental change in how companies handle their customer interactions is needed. Businesses can create lasting success in a customer-driven market by putting a premium on personalization, using AI to create memorable experiences, and upholding moral principles.

CHAPTER TEN

CONSTRUCTING AN IMPROVED FUTURE

The burden of creating a better future in a world that is becoming more interconnected and changing quickly falls on a variety of sectors, educational institutions, and individual actions. This chapter examines the critical roles that cooperation, learning, impact assessment, and proactive actions will play in creating a future that is more sustainable, just, and prosperous.

10.1 Cooperation with Industry

Innovation and the resolution of complex global challenges require cross-industry collaboration. The most important issues facing the globe cannot be resolved by one person acting alone; instead, a team effort utilizing a variety of knowledge, assets, and viewpoints is needed.

- **Breaking Down Silos:** Industries have historically

worked in isolated silos, concentrating on their specialized fields with little to no connection with one another. Nevertheless, these silos are becoming more and more ineffective in the modern global economy. Breaking down these obstacles to promote cross-sector alliances that can address complex issues like digital transformation, healthcare, and climate change is part of industry collaboration. For instance, tech companies and healthcare providers may work together to create innovative digital health solutions, while energy companies and environmental organizations could combine to promote sustainable practices.

- **Creativity Through Partnership:** By combining diverse viewpoints and areas of expertise, collaboration encourages creativity. Collaboratively, companies can build solutions that would be unfeasible to produce alone. For example, supply chains have been streamlined by collaborations between retail and logistics companies, saving costs and increasing efficiency, while the car industry's cooperation with tech companies has resulted in advances in autonomous driving technology.

- **Shared Resources and Knowledge:** Research data, technology, infrastructure, and other resources are frequently shared as part of industry collaboration. This sharing speeds up development while simultaneously cutting expenses. Companies can obtain economies of scale and access to cutting-edge technologies and insights that would be too costly or complex to develop separately by pooling their resources. The pharmaceutical industry is a prime example, as businesses frequently work together to do research and development for novel medications, sharing the substantial expenses and risks involved in this process.

- **Taking on International Challenges:** Numerous modern issues, like environmental sustainability, call for a coordinated response from several different industries. By working together, industries are able to coordinate their efforts and develop all-encompassing solutions that deal with the underlying issues rather than simply their symptoms.

For instance, in order to develop sustainable alternatives and recycling programs, the packaging industry, waste management firms, manufacturers of consumer goods, and governments must work together to combat plastic pollution.

10.2 Training and Education

The cornerstones of creating a better future are training and education. The requirement for a trained and flexible staff grows as industries change. Putting money into education and training guarantees that people have the information and abilities needed to prosper in a world that is changing quickly.

- **Continuous Learning Culture:** Due to the rapid evolution of technology, the skills needed in the workforce are ever-changing. A shift toward a culture of continuous learning, where education is not limited to formal institutions but rather a lifetime endeavor, is necessary to keep up. Through workshops, online courses, and professional certifications, businesses should support and encourage their employees' continuous learning and skill development. This methodology not only facilitates employees' continued relevance but also amplifies corporate creativity and agility.

- **Closing the Competency Divide:** The abilities required in the workplace and those taught in educational institutions frequently diverge. To narrow this gap, educators and business leaders must work together more closely to create curricula that accurately represent the demands of the labor market both now and in the future. For instance, colleges and technical institutes may collaborate with digital firms to create curricula that teach data science, cybersecurity, or coding—skills that are in great demand but frequently undersupplied.

- **STEM Education Promotion:** Science, technology, engineering, and mathematics (STEM) education is vital because technology is still at the center of practically every industry. Promoting STEM education among youth, particularly those from underrepresented groups, will contribute to the development of a skilled and diverse workforce that can lead innovation. Programs like robotics clubs, coding boot camps, and STEM scholarships can be quite effective in generating interest in and facilitating access to these important professions.

- **Retraining and Enhancement:** Many traditional vocations are changing or going out of style as automation and artificial intelligence increase. Programs for reskilling and upskilling are crucial to ensuring that workers are not left behind. Through these programs, workers can acquire new skills that are in line with the demands of the contemporary market. A factory worker may receive training in modern manufacturing methods or programming, for instance, which would allow them to move into positions that are less vulnerable to automation.

10.3 Assessing Effect

Measuring the results of projects and efforts is crucial in the quest for a brighter future. It is impossible to know whether actions are producing the expected results or whether adjustments are required without measurement.

- **Defining KPIs (Key Performance Indicators):** Organizations must first establish relevant and unambiguous KPIs before they can monitor impact successfully. These metrics ought to be in line with the aims of the company as well as the more general societal or environmental goals that they seek to fulfill. For instance, a business that is dedicated to lowering its carbon footprint may establish KPIs for waste management, energy use, and emissions reduction.

- **Decision Making Driven by Data:** Data collection and analysis become crucial after KPIs are set. Data should be used by organizations to track developments, spot trends, and make wise decisions. This method guarantees that resources are used effectively and permits real-time modifications. Data may be utilized, for example, in a social impact effort to monitor the number of people contacted, the results attained, and the regions that require further assistance.

- **Accountability and Transparency:** Measuring impact includes more than simply internal evaluations; it also entails accountability and transparency to many stakeholders, such as consumers, staff members, investors, and the community. Organizations should share both their achievements and difficulties in their progress reports on a regular basis. This openness fosters trust and shows a sincere desire to achieve successful results. For instance, publicly available sustainability reports let businesses highlight their environmental initiatives and give stakeholders a comprehensive picture of their effects.

- **Long-Term Impact Evaluation:** While immediate results are desirable, gauging an initiative's long-term effects is essential to determining its actual efficacy. Organizations ought to think about the long-term ramifications of their decisions, particularly any unexpected ones. For instance, a business may evaluate the long-term effects of its community outreach initiatives, taking into account not only the short-term gains but also the programs' ability to effect long-term social change.

10.4 An Appeal for Input

Planning and strategy alone won't be enough to create a better future; people, businesses, and governments must all take action. The necessity of being proactive in addressing the opportunities and challenges that lie ahead is emphasized in this concluding part.

- **Empowering Individuals:** Each person may contribute to the creation of a better future. Individual acts collectively contribute to greater societal change, whether they be made through community activities, lifelong learning, or sustainable choices. It is crucial to empower individuals to take responsibility for their effect and to arm them with the information and resources necessary to do so. Giving people useful advice on how to lower their carbon footprint and raising knowledge of environmental issues, for example, can enable them to make a difference.

- **Corporate Responsibility:** Companies have a big impact on the environment and society. They must therefore accept accountability for their actions and set a good example. This entails implementing eco-friendly procedures, contributing to local communities, and guaranteeing moral business conduct. Programs for corporate social responsibility (CSR) can be an effective means for companies to give back and aid in the creation of a better future. Furthermore, as customers look more and more for ethical brands to support, businesses that place a high priority on social and environmental responsibility stand to benefit from a competitive edge.

- **Policy and Governance:** In order to build the foundation for a better future, governments and policymakers are essential. This entails passing laws that support human rights, advance sustainability, and stimulate creativity. In order to make sure that policies are inclusive and equitable, policymakers must also be sensitive to the demands of the general public. Government incentives, such as those promoting the use of renewable energy, can hasten the shift to a low-carbon economy, while STEM-focused educational initiatives can better equip the workforce for challenges of the future.

- **Global Cooperation:** Issues like global health, economic inequity, and climate change transcend national boundaries. It will take international cooperation and teamwork to address these concerns. To address issues that impact the entire globe, nations must cooperate through shared research, international agreements, and collective action. Projects like the climate change agreement in Paris show how effective international cooperation can be in solving pressing problems.

- **Motivating Next Generations:** Lastly, encouraging the following generation to take up the mantle is essential to creating a brighter future. Youth goals and values are greatly influenced by education, mentoring, and role models. We can make sure that the advancements we accomplish today continue into the future by fostering in future leaders a feeling of opportunity and accountability.

Creating a brighter future is a continuous, group endeavor that calls for participation from all facets of society. We can build a more sustainable, just, and prosperous society for future generations by working together in the business, investing in education and training, carefully assessing our effects, and issuing calls to action that strengthen people and organizations.

ABOUT THE AUTHOR

Author and thought leader in the IT field Taylor Royce is well known. He has a two-decade career and is an expert at tech trend analysis and forecasting, which enables a wide audience to understand complicated concepts.

Royce's considerable involvement in the IT industry stemmed from his passion with technology, which he developed during his computer science studies. He has extensive knowledge of the industry because of his experience in both software development and strategic consulting.

Known for his research and lucidity, he has written multiple best-selling books and contributed to esteemed tech periodicals. Translations of Royce's books throughout the world demonstrate his impact.

Royce is a well-known authority on emerging technologies and their effects on society, frequently requested as a speaker at international conferences and as a guest on tech podcasts. He promotes the development of ethical technology, emphasizing problems like data privacy and the digital divide.

In addition, with a focus on sustainable industry growth, Royce mentors upcoming tech experts and supports IT education projects. Taylor Royce is well known for his ability to combine analytical thinking with technical know-how. He sees a time when technology will ethically benefit humanity.

www.ingramcontent.com/pod-product-compliance
Lightning Source LLC
Chambersburg PA
CBHW050311230526
45471CB00005B/2125